# Brick Oven Pizza: How a Guy From Brooklyn Built His Own Wood Fired Pizza Oven

Dedicated to my lovely wife Mary Jane who puts up with all my hopes and dreams

Joe Falce
6/7/2012

This entire project started as a result of a family vacation taken back to Italy in 2006. The experience overwhelmed my senses. Having been born in Italy and migrated to the USA in 1962 as a very young child, I was very much removed from the true Italian culture and passion for its gastronomic pleasures. Don't get me wrong, I grew up in a household in which my mother was a fabulous cook and cooked each day. She would, each and every day, produce such favorites as homemade cavatelli, mouth watering eggplant and veal parmigiana as well as pasta fagioli. Well, you get the picture. The difference I quickly noticed was the quality of the ingredients and to me this was most particularly evident in the lowly peasant food; the pizza! Having grown up in Brooklyn, New York, I have had some pretty spectacular pizza in my days. I grew up on the standard high gluten stretchy dough pizza served at so many neighborhood pizzerias. I discovered that the smaller simple artisan pizzas produced from rustic Italian wood fired brick ovens yielded the most satisfying pizzas. These discs were light and soft, yet crispy with a smoky crust dabbled sparingly with tasty ripe san marzano tomatoes, fresh mozzarella, a sprinkle of salt, and a drizzle of olive oil. In a word; spectacular.

Upon returning home, I became obsessed with the thought of fabricating my own outdoor wood fired brick pizza oven. I spent countless hours studying various photos and websites. Valuable resources I discovered were the following two books, *Building a Wood-Fired Oven for Bread and Pizza by Tom Jaine* and *The Bread Builders- Hearth Loaves and Masonry Ovens by Daniel Wing and Alan Scott*. Between my research and my visual observations of existing ovens, I noticed that the basic construction was fairly simple, so I began to draw up and design my own pizza oven. What follows is my pictorial journey. I hope that this may inspire some of you to undertake a similar project and enjoy the benefits of producing a fine authentic wood fired pizza, as well as enjoying the wonderful focal point that your new wood fired oven will become when you gather with family and friends. From my personal experience, it is extremely satisfying and a true hit.

As with any project, planning is most important. Please check first with your town to see if any permits are needed. Once you have picked out the ideal spot, it is then time to get to work. A solid foundation is paramount. I started with a footprint of 5 foot by 5 foot and dug down about eight inches. I proceeded to mix 28 80 lb bags of concrete (Sakrete was a great product) and embedded steel wire mesh for use as a solid base. You can see a photo of the finished base below (figure 1).

Figure 1

When the base is fully cured, you can begin laying out your first course of cinder blocks and leveling them out. My project was basically a weekend project since I work Monday through Friday and didn't have much time when I arrived home in the evening. I studied many photos on the internet and drew out my own very simple plans. The main sketch I followed is below (figure 2).

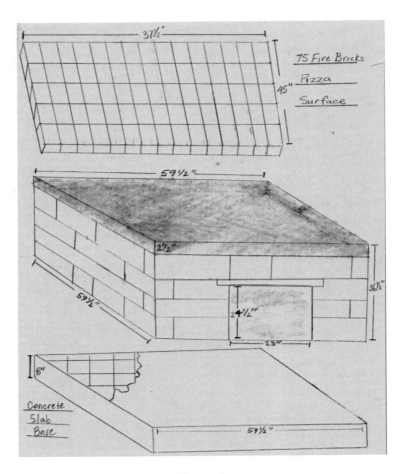

Figure 2

Planning is very important because the materials are very heavy and you will need to decide if you want to get all the materials delivered or if you want to transport them to the site yourself. I was fortunate enough to have a pick-up truck and used it to make several trips to my local mason supply and home improvement center. I have included a list of the materials (figure 3) that I used in my project along with the costs associated (note that these are 2009 prices from Long Island, New York).

| Item | Quantity | Cost /Unit | Total Cost | Comments |
|---|---|---|---|---|
| Fire Bricks | 250 | 1.09 | 296.00 | |
| 3/8" x 48" Rebar | 19 | 3.09 | 58.71 | |
| Concrete Mix - structure | 37 | 3.66 | 135.42 | 80 Lb Bag |
| Concrete Mix - base pad | 28 | 3.66 | 102.48 | 80 Lb Bag |
| 2X4 Studs | 4 | 2.07 | 8.28 | |
| Angle Brackets | 8 | 0.51 | 4.08 | For making hearth form |
| 1/2" x 10" Rebar | 3 | 6.70 | 20.10 | |
| Mortar Mix | 30 | 4.17 | 128.72 | 60 Lb Bag |
| 7" Masonry Wheels | 1 | 2.97 | 2.97 | |
| 1/2" x 18" Rebar | 18 | 1.66 | 29.88 | |
| 6"x8"x16" Block | 44 | 1.30 | 57.20 | |
| lintels 2" x 48" | 2 | 10.00 | 20.00 | |
| Refractory Mortar | 9 | 16.99 | 152.91 | 10lb container for joining fire brick |
| 4'x8' sheet plywood | 2 | 10.68 | 21.36 | for roof |
| drip edge molding | 3 | 3.78 | 11.34 | roof edge |
| Concrete mesh | 1 | 9.79 | 9.79 | for reinforcing base |
| Lathe Diamond mesh | 7 | 8.56 | 59.92 | for stucco |
| ceiling boxes | 2 | 2.17 | 4.34 | for lighting |
| 2-1/2" x 8" metal studs | 20 | 2.78 | 55.60 | |
| cement board | 9 | 6.78 | 61.02 | |
| screws for cement board | 1 | 7.47 | 7.47 | |
| asst screws & fasteners | | | 30.00 | |
| tiles | | | 28.38 | |
| Sakrete cement dye | 7 | 5.17 | 36.19 | color buff |
| Oven Thermometer | | | 18.00 | |
| Misc | | | 100.00 | chicken wire, insulating blanket etc |
| lamps | 2 | 19.98 | 39.96 | |
| roof tiles | 40 | 6.50 | 260.00 | purchased via craigslist |
| | | | 1,760.12 | |

Figure 3

Laying the first course of cinder blocks is a very exciting and anxious experience. I say this because, at least for me, you have reached the point of no return. You have committed money and lots of future time and sweat. I consider myself reasonably handy, but there were times during this project that I could hear the voice in the back of my head saying "what did you get involved with"? If you reach this point also, my advice is to take a step back and to refocus on the end product. Believe me, it will be worth it. By no means am I a mason or a bricklayer but it was here that I needed to be very patient relying heavily on my pointed trowel and my level. This is the point where the sketches and the picture in your mind's eye actually meet the pavement (figure 4).

Figure 4

You will be required to make several cuts on the cinder blocks to obtain the proper base dimensions so a good masonry blade added to a circular saw will do the trick. As with any power tools, make sure to wear the proper eye protection at all times. A mask is a good idea as there will be lots of flying dust from the cutting (figure 5).

Figure 5

I kept checking for plumb and level as I went from course to course on my cinder block base. When I got to the third course of blocks it was time to install the lentil which would support the fourth course of cinder blocks used above the opening for the firewood storage chamber. I used a 4 foot lentil which I cut in half and mortared into place (figure 6).

Figure 6

After the fourth course was completed, I allowed the base to cure and since I was only working on weekends, it was set up quite nicely for the next step (figure 7). The next step was to fill all of the cinder block chambers using concrete and rebar to tie the structure together. When the concrete and rebar filled chambers dried, it was time to measure down 2 ½" from the inside lip of the cinder blocks and mark the circumference of the interior. This mark is where I secured the platform used to support the plywood base on which I poured the concrete hearth pad. Below the 2" x 4" frame I used 4" x 4" posts cut to fit beneath the frame to the ground below. I chose to leave these in place after the concrete dried for extra support. You will note though that in the photo below (figure 8), I installed temporary braces which were knocked out of position once the concrete hearth base was completely dry and the forms were removed.

Figure 7

Figure 8

From the photo below (figure 9) you can see that all the chambers have been filled with concrete and we are ready to install the plywood platform that will act as a form base to support the concrete hearth. Note that I secured the 2"x 4" stud framing to the insides of the cinder block after the concrete had completely dried in the hollows of the blocks. I used Remington 22 caliber charges with 2" fasteners and this gave a real solid hold.

Figure 9

Now I was ready to secure the plywood base to the stud framework. I attached the plywood base using common drywall screws and I used caulking all around the plywood to create a continuous seal for the concrete that I would be pouring. You can really see the temporary support braces from the photo below (figure 10). The next step was the placement of the 4 foot rebar in a grid pattern used to reinforce the concrete hearth base. I used nylon zip cords to secure the rebar where they intersected. Once I completed the placement of the rebar, I was ready to install the form. I constructed the form by using 2" x 8" studs to which I had drew a line along the length of each of the four pieces 2 ½" down from the edge. I then installed L brackets at these lines at various points within the four boards so I could lay these on the upper lip of the cinder blocks encircling the entire diameter. Once the concrete form was in place, I sprayed the entire interior of the wood form with cooking spray as I feel this would make it easier to remove the forms once the concrete had set up (figure 11).

Figure 10

Figure 11

Here is where a good cement mixer will save a lot of time and a lot of hand mixing. I was fortunate enough to have a neighbor who had one (figure 12) and he was willing to let me use it. Using the electric cement mixer, I was able to mix 23 80 lb bags of Sakrete in about an hour and a half. This was a great time savings and it only cost me a few beers!

Figure 12

Because the concrete is mixed so quickly in the mixer, it's a good idea to call in a favor here from a good friend (I had my cousin Joe help out here) so one person could keep the mixer loaded with concrete mix and the other person can take the mixed concrete in five gallon pails and pour it into the form. This process needs to happen fluidly as you don't want the concrete to set up before you complete the entire pouring (figure 13). After all the concrete has been poured and leveled within the form (figure 14), you will need to keep the mix misted for a few days and covered with plastic sheeting until the base is fully cured. Once again, since I only worked on weekends, my base was totally dried when I removed the forms the following weekend. I feel this step is very important and you should definitely allow for the concrete to cure as slowly as possible since this will basically be supporting the majority of the weight of the brick oven. Take this step slow and serious!

Figure 13

Figure 14

After the base had thoroughly cured, I removed the form. The form came apart easily, I believe, because I had applied the cooking spray along the inside surface liberally. The next step was to begin the layout of the firebrick cooking surface, or the hearth above the just completed poured concrete base. I laid out the firebrick in soldier style on the base (figure 15) to dry fit them in the final location. It took some adjusting to get the hearth properly centered, but the time spent here will make the following steps much easier. All the constant leveling becomes evident here when you lay the fire bricks down. Remember, this will now be the inside cooking service of your pizza oven and you don't want it to be too low or too high. I found that a good general height for all to use is 39 ½". Once I was satisfied with the position of the dry laid bricks of the hearth, I swept DRY refractory mortar into all the joints and then brushed away all the excess from the surface and misted the entire area with water from a spray bottle. When this step was completed, I covered the surface overnight and was ready for the next step which was to begin the layout of the back wall of the brick oven (figure 16).

Figure 15

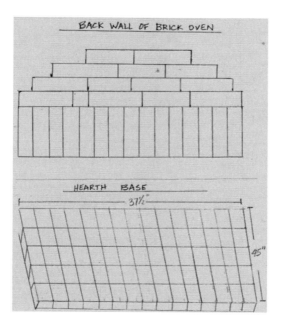

(Figure 16)

I dry set the back wall bricks in exactly the same pattern as above to check for fit. Once I was satisfied with the way they looked on the base, I began to set them together using the refractory mortar exactly as per the directions on the container. I realized that you didn't need to make a really wide joint using the refractory mortar as it is of a very fine texture and has exceptional adhering qualities. Please be sure to wear proper respiratory devices as the packaging indicates that you should avoid inhaling the product. After I allowed the back wall to completely set up overnight, I began to dry set the side walls of the oven using the diagram I laid out below (figure 17).

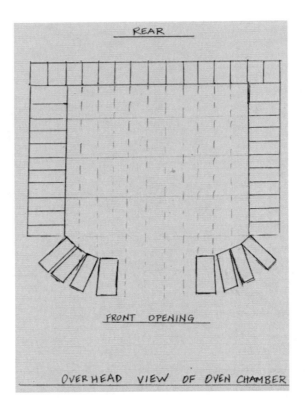

(Figure 17)

Below you can see that I really got "into" building my oven (figure 18)! I found that in order to really get a good joint I needed to actually press the mortar into all the small crevices and the best way to do this was from inside.

(Figure 18)

From the above photo, I experimented by using recycled red brick for the opening but I changed my mind for the end product. A great tool to have for the rest of the brick setting was a good electric brick saw (figure 19). You should consider renting one if you do not own one as you will need to make several bevel cuts on which the archway bricks will rest. Before you plot your bevel cuts, you will need to construct an archway jig. I found the easiest way to do this was to cut a piece of cardboard the exact width of the inside of the oven opening at the rear. I also cut the cardboard to the highest point of the rear of the oven wall. When I cut out the

cardboard as just described, I laid it on the ground and set 14 bricks in an arch pattern tracing the inside bottom with a sharpie onto the cardboard to make a template. I also made a mark at each point where two bricks met. I then removed the bricks and cut the cardboard along the line I had made. The next step was to transfer this template onto two pieces of plywood and screw them on to either side of two small lengths of 2"x4" (figure 20).

(Figure 19)

(Figure 20)

Now that the archway template was completed and set in place as in figure 20, I inserted small scraps of plywood underneath the feet of the form so that they could be easily slid out after the brick arch was set so the form could be moved forward for the next course. This process is repeated three times until I was

18

to the front of the oven. When the form is in the proper position to the rear of the oven, you can begin to lay the 14 bricks on top of the archway as illustrated. The two supporting bricks, one on either end will need to be marked and bevel cut (figure 21).

(Figure 21)

You can see from the photo below how the bevel cut bricks will be set onto the top of the sidewall bricks and will support the archway bricks (figure 22). Note also that I dry fit the lentil that will support the bricks at the opening of the oven chamber.

(Figure 22)

The photo below (figure 23) shows good progress with the first course of the archway set in place with the refractory cement and the form now moved forward to support the fabrication of the second course of bricks in the dome of the oven. Note that the height of the dome is approximately 16" at the highest point. There is a ratio that must be followed for proper convection in the oven. A 16" dome height required a maximum door height of 10" as a result of my internet investigation. This translates to a door height ratio of approximately 62.5% of the dome height. Once again I found it necessary to employ not only a trowel, but also my fingers to make sure that the refractory mortar was properly applied to all joints. When all three archway courses were completed, I covered the structure with a plastic drop cloth and allowed it to set up until the next weekend. This project as you can tell by now requires long intervals between certain steps in order to achieve the anticipated results. Patience is certainly a virtue when you are constructing your pizza oven as each step directly affects the following step so you want to make sure that you are doing it right or else you will be dismantling something and wasting more time and more money. I found that I only focused on the end product. I had a vision in my mind's eye of what the finished product would look like and of all the fun it would be for my family and friends. This is what you should focus on; take your time!

(Figure 23)

The next photo gives you a side view of the three arches completed. The arch support was removed as soon as the last arch was completely dry. At this point I started calling upon my high school geometry as I needed to make custom cuts in order to close the front dome of the oven. This step was tedious and time consuming. I searched many websites and photos and videos of what others had done here, but I found that trial and error as well as small cardboard templates worked extremely well in determining the shape of cut I needed to make to fill the gaps and close the dome. Aesthetics are not important here as this will be completely concealed under several inches of concrete and insulation. I used a pipe clamp to do the center three brick rows first (you can see the clamp in figure 24). The lower brick is cut to fit in the channel of the lentil above the bricks framing the oven opening. Next the keystone bricks are carefully cut. It may take several passes to achieve the results you need to slide down and lock the front of the last arch to the back side of the brick reaching down to the lentil of the oven opening. Take your time again here and make your cuts as minimal as possible. Like I mentioned earlier, I set three courses side by side here and then used the pipe clamp to hold it together until it was dry. Once these three courses were dry, I removed the pipe clamp and proceeded to work my way out to either side until all openings to the oven were sealed, albeit the oven door opening.

(Figure 24)

Below is a photo showing the completed sides of the dome. You will also note a steel pipe protruding from the upper left side, this is the channel that the probe for my oven thermometer to pass through (figure 25). You will note off to the side the miscellaneous cuts of brick as I attempted to achieve the proper angles to fill the spaces. I often found myself asking: "What shall I use to fill the empty spaces"? Hey didn't Pink Floyd say that? Sorry, that was bad. Anyway, you will also note from the photo (figure 26) that I changed the forward facing bricks from the recycled red brick experiment, to the same style fire brick that I used throughout the construction.

(Figure 25)

(Figure 26)

The photo below (figure 27) is of the front opening looking up past the lentil supporting the front course of bricks and up to the dome. This is the view that the pizza sees.

(Figure 27)

From the photo below (figure 28), you will see how I have made a lot of progress. I have used granite tiles cut to size to cover over bricks that I had set onto the concrete hearth base. Once this granite base was completely dry, I stacked the forward facing fire bricks which would act as the support for the front archway. The front archway bricks are actually half-cut bricks in order to allow additional space behind them to act as the chimney flue passage way. You will also note that I constructed a second archway template in the exact fashion I had described earlier for the main chamber arches.

(Figure 28)

Now you can really see the oven taking shape below (figure 29). You can now see the side profile revealing the half cut bricks in front of the oven opening and the pipe extensions for the oven thermometer probe. At this point, I also laid a layer of chicken wire over the archway of the oven. Also I have begun to cover the refractory mortar with regular mortar. I then cut two lengths of angle iron and placed them parallel behind the front archway and in front and above the oven opening lentil. I then cut a piece of cement board to lie between these two angle irons. When I was satisfied with the fit of the cement board, I removed it and placed it on the ground and laid my terra cotta 8" x 36" chimney flue pipe section on top of it. I proceeded to trace the *inside* opening with a Sharpie and then I cut out this opening using a jig saw. I then placed the cut cement board back into the angle iron channel I had created and filled this area with concrete to hold everything in place. The next step was to build a plywood form (figure 30) all the way around the oven 4" out. This chamber will be filled with concrete and allowed to dry for at least one week. I added strips of wood extending side to side in order to keep the forms from pushing outward. The strips can later be cut back in order to remove the forms.

(Figure 29)

(Figure 30)

Now with the form removed, you can see the totally encased oven (figure 31). This oven is both solid and efficient at this point ready to withstand the wide temperature swings and to maintain the heat. In later steps, I will further increase the heat

26

retention capability by filling the final enclosure with an insulating blanket as well as vermiculite that I had removed from the base of the above ground pool I had discarded to make room for this pizza oven project.

(Figure 31)

Below is a front view of the oven (figure 32). You can better see the ends of the angle irons buried now in solid concrete and supporting the first course of flue pipe. Technically, the oven is functional now and the following steps are more for aesthetic purposes. At this point you can basically finish the oven any way you wish. You could choose to just paint the entire structure, decorate it with tiles or do decorative stone work. You can be as creative as you like. I, myself pictured a gathering point. A point where my family and friends could feel part of the experience and get involved in the fun that a pizza party really is! Think about it, ever since we were little children, the mention of a pizza party evokes a pleasant and festive feeling for us all. With this in mind, I drew up a structure that resembled a *home* so to speak, with a working chimney, a tiled roof and decorative lighting. But again, on your oven, be as creative as you like and place your own stamp upon it.

(Figure 32)

To create a "house-like" structure, I needed to put up side walls which would eventually house the oven, contain the insulation and support the roof. Below, I am drilling the holes into the concrete hearth base (figure 33) that would receive the lead anchors that would secure the metal studs to which the cement board would be secured. I used a scrap piece of cement board to act as the outer edge of the upper wall which would be flush and plumb to the bottom cinder block support. I used a small section of metal stud behind the scrap of cement board and then I used a Sharpie to mark off lines for the rear-most edge of the stud around the entire circumference of the structure.

(Figure 33)

After I secured the lower metal studs to the hearth base, I began to encase the entire structure with metal studs spaced at 16" intervals (figure 34).

(Figure 34)

Notice that to secure the metal stud around the brick archway, I used relieve cuts using tin snips. I used concrete screws to anchor the stud into the mortar joints. The next step was to cut and screw the cement board to the metal studs (figure 35). Note below the view from above and inside the chamber now created when the cement boards have been screwed on to create an outer wall.

(Figure 35)

Below the concrete that encases the brick oven has been covered by an insulating blanket. I used some left over air conditioning insulation made for duct work (figure 36). On top of the insulating blanket, I used vermiculite. I had reclaimed and recycled the vermiculite (figure 37) from the base of an above ground pool that used to occupy the space now occupied by the oven. Waste not, want not is something I learned at a very young age.

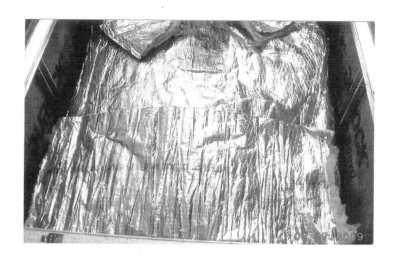

(Figure 36)

(Figure 37)

I cut a hole into the cement board to accept the oven thermometer and inserted the probe part into the pipe that I had cemented into the oven chamber. Above the cement board I installed the roof gables at an approximate 20 degree angle (figure 38). I am no mathematician, but based on my calculation of roughly a 4 ½" rise per 12" horizontal run, that works out to be about a 20.525 degrees pitch. Once the roof framing was completed, I cut the cement board to attach it to the studs to complete the front and back façade of the structure. The next step was to cover the common rafters which I had lashed together for added stability. I did this by using a section of a metal stud which I cut end to end using a tin snip to fashion a flat strip. A good picture of this strip is below (figure 39). I made up this step as I felt it would tie the entire roof structure together. Also, note that I added additional vermiculite at this stage to increase the oven's insulating property. I used ¾" exterior grade plywood to cover the structure and covered that with tar paper in preparation for the roof tiles.

(Figure 38)

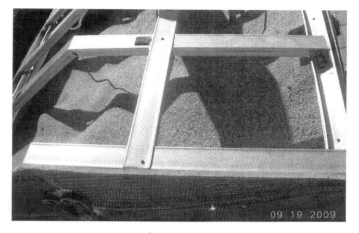

(Figure 39)

Also visible in figure 39, you can see how I attached the roof rafters to the roof plate using L brackets that I fashioned from strips of metal left over from the metal studs I used. At this point, I just couldn't wait any more so I lit the first small fire in the oven begin the full curing and seasoning process (figure 40).

(Figure 40)

I lit the fire by using some rolled up newspaper and kindling made from small dried-out branches. When the fire was going, I added some larger split hardwood pieces (figure 41) and let it burn until the soot was burned off of the interior oven dome. I fed the fire for roughly one hour and then let it die out slowly on its own. I repeated this process every other night for the next two weeks.

(Figure 41)

Note in the above photo that the chimney flue is still not completed to its finished height (an additional 3 foot length will be added when the roofing and tiles are added). Also note that I have drawn circles on either upper outer corner of the oven. These circles will be cut out to accept round electrical boxed used for my decorative lighting. The switch box will be affixed to the lower left side of the structure. I took this opportunity to wire the switch to the two round boxes. I will supply power to the circuit at a later date, but for now the wiring has been completed allowing me to put on the roof. The entire structure, except for the roof of course was covered with wire lathe to accept the stucco coat which I chose to clad my oven. Note from the photo below (figure 42) that many changes have taken place. For example, you can see that the additional 3 foot length of terra cotta chimney flue has been added. You can see that the plywood roofing sheeting has been secured to the rafters and covered with tar paper. The roof edge drip molding has been nailed in place. The electrical switch box has been wired to the two decorative lighting round boxes (covered by cardboard to prevent stucco from getting into the boxes). The decorative tiles have been affixed and you can see that a scratch coat of the stucco is being applied. You can also see that masking tape has been applied to protect the bricks and granite edges from the stucco application process.

(Figure 42)

At this point it was time to mix the mortar stucco using the colorant to achieve the proper intensity of color hue that you desire. Sakrete makes a Quikrete product called "Liquid Cement Color". It comes in a 10 ounce plastic container and is sold in home improvement centers next to the Quikrete. I used the color called BUFF for my oven. When you are mixing your own, please make note of the ratio of Liquid color to the mortar mix bags that you are mixing and follow this ratio for each batch that you make. Below (figure 43) I am applying the stucco using a hawk and a flat 10" hand trowel.

(Figure 43)

It is important to work fast here as you want to avoid the stucco from setting up before the entire mixed batch has been applied. This would lead to unnecessary waste, so only mix what you can apply without interruptions. If you complete one section, you can always apply another section at a later date. Below is the structure with the stucco completely applied (figure 44).

(Figure 44)

Now that the structure was dry, I attached the light fixtures to the round boxes that I had already installed. Below is a photo showing the lighting fixtures that I selected and installed (figure 45). These lights add both form and function. I believe they blend well with the Tuscan style motif and the light that they provide when I am making pizzas at night makes them functional.

(Figure 45)

I was lucky enough to find the roofing tiles locally via a *Craigslist* ad. I had been having problems in purchasing quantities less than a pallet. If you look long and hard enough you can find just about anything. The composite roofing tiles that I was able to purchase were a left over quantity of a terra cotta and composite tile that I screwed down to the plywood using a pre-drilled hole in each tile and then I mortared each joint for strength and uniformity. I have added a side view (figure 46) and a front view (figure 47).

(Figure 46)

(Figure 47)

In order to run electric to power the lights, I added a functional counter space (figure 48) which allowed me to pass the electrical conduit supplying power to the switch/lights, a functional sink with hot and cold running water for easy clean ups as well as a refrigerator to store the toppings in the warm summer months. Note that I painted the roof mortar joints to create a more flowing look to the entire structure.

(Figure 48)

I fabricated a wooden door to seal the oven opening in between uses. At this point, I was ready to make my first pizza! Invest in a good digital scale as I found that a dough ball formed at 330 grams yields a nice 10" pizza which is perfectly suited for my oven. Below is a recipe for pizza dough and basic pizza sauce that I use for my margherita pie (note that I accounted for 11 doughs which I found makes for a great pizza party!)

### Basic Dough (yields 11 330 gram doughs)

14 cups of all purpose flour (you can use the Caputo 00 if you can find it)

5 cups of water

4 teaspoons of salt

1 cup of olive oil

4 teaspoons of active dry yeast

Pinch of sugar

Place 1 cup of lukewarm water in a stainless steel mixing bowl sprinkle in the yeast, add the pinch of sugar and cover with plastic wrap for 5 minutes.

Place the flour and salt in a very, very large stainless steel bowl make a well in the center and pour in the yeast. Add the olive oil and the remaining oil and continue to hand mix until the dough is well mixed together.

Gather the dough into a large ball and remove from the mixing bowl and place on a well floured surface. Continue to kneed the dough until it becomes smooth and elastic, about 10 minutes.

Place this ball back into a large oiled bowl and cover with plastic wrap for at least 3 hours ,allowing to rise.

Remove the risen dough, punch it down and work it into 330 gram balls, handling as little as possible as to not lose the small fermentation air bubbles that occur in the dough. Once the individual dough balls have been formed, you can lay these out in a covered container, in individual plastic bags that can be refrigerated for up to a week or you can just shape them into your 10" pizza after they have rested for at least 1 hour.

If you are ready to make pizzas, you can spread a little flour or cornmeal on a wooden pizza peel and shape your pizza right on the peel. I add the pizza sauce (see recipe below) very sparingly to about one inch from the edges of the pizza. I break off small chunks of the fresh mozzarella and spread it on top of the sauce. I then drizzle just a bit of olive oil, a pinch of salt and it is now ready for its quick 2 to 3 minutes in the well heated pizza oven. You will need to use a metal pizza peel to monitor and turn the pizza in the oven so you can evenly cook the pizza all around.

## Simple basic Margherita Pizza Sauce

One 28 ounce can of Whole San Marzano tomatos

Pinch of salt

Remove the stems and seeds from the tomatoes and hand crush into a container that you can latter ladle onto formed pizza dough.

(Figure 49)

Above is a very simple and tasty margherita pie being constructed (figure 49). Below is the pizza being loaded into the oven to undergo its delicious and swift baking (figure 50).

(Figure 50)

Below is the pizza actually cooking in the well heated oven (figure 51). The temperature can get to well over 800 degrees when the oven has been thoroughly heated. It is very, very important to turn the pizza quickly otherwise the side closest to the fire will quickly blister and quite likely burn if you do not keep it moving.

(Figure 51)

A perfectly cooked pizza just being removed from the oven (figure 52), this is where all the hard work pays off with a crisp smoky on the outside with a light airy and chewy inside crust mate with the simple toppings to produce sheer heaven!

(Figure 52)

The actual pizza oven becomes just a backdrop. I feel, at least in my case, that the oven is an excuse to gather family and close friends. I feel strongly that in today's hectic times, we truly have lost sight of what is really important and that is enjoying family and friends over a simple meal. I see how the oven acts like an immediate magnet for my guests and everyone wants to get involved and shares in the good cheer. There is always a lot of laughing and the time seems to slip away very quickly. At the end of the evening, I always hear "We must do this again real soon". To me this always reinforces the fact that my project was a true success!

Below are some additional pizza recipes which are all based off the basic dough recipe outlined earlier with toppings that I have found to be very popular:

**New York Style Pizza Pie**

Begin by stretching out the basic dough from the recipe I provided earlier on a floured pizza peel. Add one ladle, about 3 oz of your favorite tomato sauce and spread evenly. Add shredded mozzarella cheese a pinch of oregano, a pinch of grated Romano cheese and a light drizzle of olive oil.

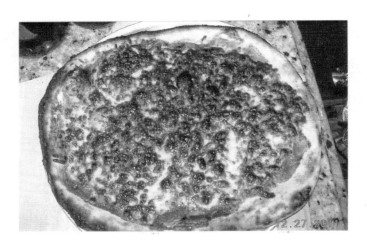

## Pepperoni Pizza

Use the basic dough recipe provided earlier, then you add 3 oz of your favorite tomato sauce, you can either add sliced fresh mozzarella or you can use shredded mozzarella. You then need to add sliced pepperoni.

### Clam Pizza Pie

Begin by stretching out the basic dough from the recipe I provided earlier on a floured pizza peel. Here I like to use a deli sliced low moisture mozzarella laid out on the stretched out dough to about ½" from the edges, I use this method because I find that the clams sometimes contain too much water and if you don't put the cheese below the clams, they tend to soak through the dough in the cooking process thus preventing the formation of a crispy pie. I then add 1 dozen fresh shucked little neck clams that have been marinated in white wine. I spread the clams over the mozzarella and then add a light drizzle of olive oil and thinly sliced garlic and oregano.

## Pesto Pizza Pie

Begin by stretching out the basic dough from the recipe I provided earlier on a floured pizza peel. Then spread out about 3 oz of ricotta cheese and top with your favorite pesto.

## **Porcini Mushrooms with Kalamata Olives and Red Onion**

Begin by stretching out the basic dough from the recipe I provided earlier on a floured pizza peel. Slice about 2 or 3oz of porcini mushrooms (you can use re-constituted dried porcini mushrooms also) and spread over your dough, then slice about 12 kalamata olives and spread them over the mushrooms, top this with red onion slices and drizzle with olive oil.

## Anchovy and Capers Pizza Pie

Begin by stretching out the basic dough from the recipe I provided earlier on a floured pizza peel. Ladle out 3 oz of your favorite marinara sauce and distribute one small can of flat anchovy fillets in olive oil and 1 tablespoon of capers.

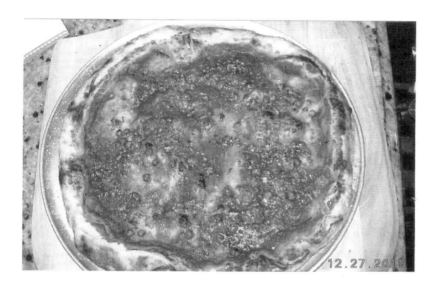

Made in United States
North Haven, CT
14 February 2023

32577369R00030